The Essential
Book of
DREAMS

The Essential
Book of
DREAMS

JACKUM BROWN

MOON
STONE

First published in Great Britain in 2000 by
Michael O'Mara Books Limited
9 Lion Yard
Tremadoc Road
London SW4 7NQ

ISBN 1-85479-511-2
A CIP catalogue record of this book is available from the British
Library

13579108642
Designed and typeset by Design 23

Printed and bound in Great Britain by
Cox and Wyman Limited, Reading, Berks.

We are such stuff as dreams are made on, and our little life is rounded with a sleep.

William Shakespeare

THE TEMPEST

INTRODUCTION

Sleep is an essential part of our lives –
we all spend nearly a third of our time
sleeping, and we all spend part of our
sleeping time dreaming. People have
always been fascinated by dreams and
their meanings – some of the earliest
recorded dreams come from ancient
Egypt, around four thousand years ago.
One such is even engraved in
hieroglyphics between the paws of the
Sphinx.

Most ancient cultures set great store by
dreams – they were thought to be
messages from their gods or from their
ancestors. Egyptians, Greeks, Romans,
Chinese and Japanese all built dream
temples and the priests and priestesses

attached to the temples were held in high regard. People came to have their dreams interpreted, and to have their minds and bodies healed.

In other parts of the world, such as Africa, Asia and North and South America, shamanism was, and indeed still is, practised. Training to become a shaman is an extremely lengthy and arduous process during which altered states of consciousness must be fully explored. Dreaming is one such state and the initiate learns not only to control and direct his own dreams, but also how to use his knowledge to help, heal and advise others.

In Australia, Aborigines believe the whole world was created in Dreamtime and that everything that has yet to be discovered or invented lives under the Earth's surface waiting to be dreamed into existence. The Bushmen of the Kalahari believe the whole of life to be a dream and that life, somehow, is dreaming them.

Native North Americans believed that each person, prior to their birth, had their own Great Dream which conferred various good qualities upon them. Sadly the Dream was forgotten as they emerged into life. Catching and interpreting their dreams was a way of life for most tribes. There were initiation rites involving each young warrior in the search for his Great Dream and there are still ceremonies where dreams are ritually acted out.

Dream catching meant forming a magic circle around yourself in which you captured messages from your dream Spirit. The pretty dream catchers that you can buy today are a physical interpretation of this magic circle. In their purest form they also represent a modern dream of a way of life that is more in touch with the natural world and less entranced with materialism.

More recently the great psychoanalysts, Sigmund Freud and Carl Gustav Jung worked hard on dreams. Freud's work emphasised a sexual interpretation of dreams. He believed that humans are basically driven by their instinct for survival, and that sex is therefore our prime motivation. He felt that only in dreams can people express their true thoughts and desires without the self-censorship that we all bring to our waking lives. Jung's work was more holistic in nature. He theorised that we each have masculine and feminine elements in our psyches, known as the animus and the anima, and that they should be balanced. He believed that dreams help us to achieve our full potential by tapping into the vast reservoir of the whole of human experience – if only they are correctly analysed and interpreted.

Dreams are clearly useful to us all, and this book hopes to explain how we can try to harness them in such a way as to bring a better sense of perspective and balance to our lives.

WHAT ARE DREAMS?

*Dreams, sir, are awkward
and confusing things:
not all that people see in
them comes true.*

Homer
THE ODYSSEY

When we dream, we are talking to ourselves. Current thinking suggests that often the figures inhabiting our dreams are also ourselves. Our unconscious minds can cut through the layers of civilisation that are imposed on us all from infancy, tossing aside accepted mores and telling us what we truly think and feel, regardless of how much we repress this knowledge in our daily lives.

Today, western civilisation has largely lost its knowledge of dreams, so much so that most people think of dream working as complete nonsense. They should give some thought to the absolute fact that research in sleep laboratories shows that people who are deprived of their dreamtime soon become disorientated, anxious, aggressive and eventually show signs of psychosis.

DEEP SLEEP AND REM

During our sleep we alternate between periods of deep sleep and slow brain activity and what is known as REM or rapid eye movement. It is during the REM time that we do most of our dreaming, and periods of REM become longer as the night goes on. The tiredness we feel following a bad night's sleep may have more to do with being deprived of dreamtime than physical exhaustion, as our bodies can rest without actually sleeping.

We need sleep when we are babies and babies certainly dream. This can be seen by their REM time. We need sleep when we are ill – it is undoubtedly the body's automatic response to being under attack, and it is during sleep that our immune systems get to work to repair the damage. We know that we need to dream because when we do not we quickly begin to suffer, so it seems logical to assume that dreams are a part of the healing process too.

Many books have been written on the subject of dreams, ranging from the extremely serious to the frivolous. The kind of interpretation of dreams that you are likely to do for yourself at home, and the self-knowledge and self-help you can achieve, will probably fall somewhere in the middle. Books can only help you so much. Dictionaries of dream symbols can be very helpful, but in a general way. In the end you must always use your own intuition.

Bear in mind that some people, places and objects will hold a special significance for you, either because of important past experiences in your life, or because of some little incident in your day that your mind has touched on just before you slept. Try to work on your interpretations in the light of your own experience of life, and use the help you find in books for what it is – help, and not truth written in stone.

·

TYPES OF DREAMS

*Dreams are true while they
last, and do we not live in
dreams?*

Alfred Lord Tennyson
THE HIGHER PANTHEISM

·

Dreams naturally fall into various distinctive types. Before you try to interpret them in any way, you need to categorise them. Many dreams are extremely straight forward – either the mind is telling us something we need to know now, or organising and filing events of the day. It is clearly a waste of time trying to read intricate meanings into these types of dream – unless, of course, they were just a small part of a larger and more complex dream.

INSTINCTIVE NEED DREAMS

The simplest type can be called Instinctive Need dreams. These are tied into your physical state – your body's needs. For example, if you dream that you are very thirsty, you are quite likely to wake up and find that you are indeed very thirsty. Dream of finding yourself on an ice floe in the Arctic ocean and you have probably kicked off your duvet. Dream of boiling under the desert sun and find you forgot to turn off the central heating before you went to bed.

My own family were very fond of discussing their dreams over the breakfast table, some of which were so memorable in one way or another that they entered our family history. One such, dreamt by my brother, aged about twelve, was that he was asleep but desperate to go to the loo. So, in his dream, he got out of bed and went off to the bathroom. When he lifted the loo seat a deep voice rang out from the bottom of the bowl 'Squad, halt!' Apart from being quite an amusing dream, it not only tells of physical need on his part but also of his awareness that he was, in fact, still asleep and in his bed.

LITERAL DREAMS

Literal dreams are the sort of dreams where you are running through all the events of the day, however mundane. Your mind is literally digesting all the information that your five senses have experienced while you were awake. It is thought that in this way the mind sorts, stores and cross references information. These are usually dreams that you remember in disconnected fragments, and they are often perfectly logical. Sometimes, particularly if you have spent the day doing something repetitive although not something you usually do, e.g. decorating a room, you seem to spend the whole night wielding the paintbrush too!

However, you are just as likely to have to follow a chain that your dream has triggered. For example, let us say that you dream about someone who attended the same evening class as you did last year, even though you had no contact with them that day, nor any desire to contact them. In fact, there is no obvious reason to have dreamt of them at all. Think back carefully over the events of the day that has just passed and try to find any connection, however slight, with the person you dreamt of. You might find that someone you saw in the supermarket had a similar way of walking, or the same type of hairstyle, or voice – something must have jogged your memory. This cross referencing effect is thought to be part of the mind's filing system.

WISH-FULFILMENT DREAMS

These are dreams we all have from time to time, but again, they do not often have a great deal of hidden meaning – you were probably just 'day dreaming' before you went to sleep. You might dream that you have won the lottery, or that you are a famous musician, successfully holding a large audience in the palm of your hand, or that you are strolling with your lover beneath the palm trees on some romantic, tropical island. If, however, you find you dream this kind of dream over and over again, you should begin to pay it some attention. Your mind may be trying to suggest something to you – that you should take up those piano lessons again, or that your relationship would benefit from a stress free period on neutral territory.

BALANCING AND INTEGRATIVE DREAMS

These are dreams in which our minds seem to be struggling to come to terms with emotional or psychological difficulties in our lives. As you progress through this book you will begin to see the relevance of keeping a dream diary and how it can help decipher the imagery and strong signals that the unconscious mind is sending to the sleeper. Most of the memorable and intriguing dreams we have are of this type – they often present in a weird and surreal fashion. The great French artist, Magritte, painted in a way reminiscent of this type of dream and, more recently, the lyrics of some of Bob Dylan's songs strike a chord in the language of dreams.

A friend of mine told me the following dream. He is a creative person, a composer and musician who is happily married and leading a life which pleases him. The only thing that might improve it for him would be getting more work and becoming better known. His wife is a successful business woman who deeply admires his work and is genuinely happy to be able to help nurture his talents in any way she can.

He dreamt that he was driving with his wife in an old VW beetle, with a large two-handled bin in the back that was full of orange juice.

He was worried that a lot of it would spill by the time they reached their destination. His wife was keeping an eye on the bin and kept telling him everything was fine. Suddenly one of the rear wheels on the car just came off and rolled away. The car lurched and some of the orange juice spilled. He put the wheel back on the car and his wife reassured him that not much had been spilled. He continued driving until they reached their destination.

He parked the car at the bottom of a grand set of steps that swept upwards and up which, he realised they were going to have to carry the heavy bin. My friend's wife is much smaller than he is, so her side of the bin was naturally lower than his. This made carrying the bin without spilling the orange juice very difficult, but despite an irritable exchange, they managed quite well and not a lot was lost.

At the top of the steps was a great long marble promenade, and he was tired and annoyed that they were expected to carry the bin such a long way when it was so hard to do. They carried on anyway. He kept worrying about the orange juice that was spilling and she kept telling him not to keep fussing about it. At the end of the promenade they found another huge set of stairs, which they then had to descend very carefully without spilling too much. As they reached the bottom of the stairs, he realised that the bin was still very full but then, to his dismay, he saw the VW beetle parked there...

My reading of this dream is quite different to his: he thought this dream was telling him that there was no point in arguing with his wife, because she was bound to be right. I think that at some unacknowledged level his ego was a bit bruised. He may have been feeling that some practical aspects of his relationship were unequal and that his wife was becoming somehow more in control of their life together than he was. He seems to be feeling that this was a situation that would never change. However, he was obviously also aware that between them they could overcome any difficulties they encountered on their journey together and that they had a successful partnership.

Language is often as important as imagery in our dreams. Punning, for example, and double meanings, can be watched out for. A man in his forties who was suffering from a great deal of self-doubt despite being successful and leading an apparently happy life, decided he needed therapy. He told me that early on in his treatment he dreamed that he was standing, doing nothing, in the Holloway Road in north London whilst people went about their daily business. The therapist pointed out to him that on a very basic level he might want to think about the double meaning there – Holloway/hollow way.

CREATIVE DREAMS
These dreams are much rarer than balancing dreams, and tend to have more structure – often a beginning, a middle and an end. They are the sort of extremely vivid dreams where occasionally we might find the solution to a tricky problem. An artist

might find inspiration. A writer might find the idea for a novel.

There are many, well documented examples of this type of dream. Einstein is said to have based his theory of relativity on a childhood dream. Elias Howe had been struggling with the problem of how to make a sewing machine. He could not work out how to thread the needle in such a way that it could pull the thread in and out of the material without getting completely tangled up. Finally he had a dream in which a group of ferocious savages were about to kill him and as they raised their spears he saw that each one had a hole through the point. He awoke to realise he had solved his problem. Until then he had been thinking that the hole in the needle would be at the blunt end, as it is with a hand sewing needle.

Another much quoted example of this kind of problem solving dream is that of Freidrich Kekulé von Stradonitz, the German chemist. He had been struggling to find the molecular structure of benzene over a long period of time and his mind was fully concentrated on the problem. The answer came to him in a dream, as he was asleep in a chair by the fire. He saw long chains, like snakes, twisting and turning around. Suddenly one of these snakes grabbed its own tail and whirled around in front of him. When he awoke he realised that his mind had given him a possible answer, that the atoms were arranged in a ring, rather than in a straight line. He spent the rest of the night perfecting the formula which eventually gave us the combustion engine and the motor car.

Snakes have many symbolic meanings – temptation, sin and fear, sexuality, healing and renewal, wisdom and the revelation of that which is hidden. In Kekulé von Stradonitz's case, none of these really apply – his dream was more likely to be a result of his unconscious mind applying itself to his problem and eventually finding a vivid image with which to prompt his conscious mind. It is true, of course, that the dream did reveal that which was hidden!

It is possible that Leonardo da Vinci

designed his aeroplane in response to a dream, and even that science fiction writers such as Arthur C. Clarke have been inspired in this way. *Alice in Wonderland* is full of dream symbolism. The composer Tartini had a very strong dream of the Devil playing his violin, and as a result he wrote *The Devil's Sonata*.

LUCID DREAMS

These are dreams that most of us have had from time to time. You are having a vivid dream but you are fully aware of the fact that you are dreaming. You may actually wake up in the middle of an interesting or exciting dream and decide that you want it to continue. Once again asleep but aware that you are dreaming, you can direct your dream to some extent, practise flying, for example, or indulge in a sexual encounter. In Carlos Casteneda's books about his apprenticeship to a Yacqui Indian sorcerer in Mexico, he is told to look at his hands as soon as he realises that he is dreaming. This centres him in his body and enables him to begin to control his dream.

NIGHTMARES AND RECURRING DREAMS
Nightmares can be brought about by a number of different causes, quite often physical. The food and drink you consume at night can affect your dreams, particularly if you eat late, and go to bed soon afterwards. The classic

examples are cheese and coffee, but too much alcohol can produce the same result. Alcoholics tend to have bad dreams, which can, in advanced cases, spill over into their waking state, causing delusions and paranoia. Drug addicts also suffer from nightmares. In all of these cases nightmares occur because the sleeping pattern is disturbed, either by the digestive process, or because the alcohol or drugs have put the sleeper into such a deep sleep that their REM time cannot take place correctly. As we know, loss of REM time leads to disorientation and anxiety.

Noises such as the door bell or the alarm clock sounding can trigger nightmares, as can jerking in one's sleep. The muscular spasm known as the myoclonic jerk normally occurs when just going into or coming out of sleep, but twitching during sleep is fairly common too. Worries produce anxiety dreams of which there are many common examples, e.g. your teeth all start to disintegrate in your mouth and as you try to speak you are spitting them out. Another very straightforward causes of nightmares is watching a scary film, a shocking documentary, or falling asleep reading a horror story. Sometimes, of course, nightmares occur as a result of severe stress in your waking life – often when the situation is completely out of your control, as with looming redundancy, a serious accident or illness befalling yourself or someone you love, or a recent bereavement.

This is a typical example of a serious stress dream: shortly after the tragic and unexpected death of her partner, a friend dreamt that she was lying in pieces on the floor of her living room. She realised that her eyes were on the other side of the room, and knew that if she could only reach them, she could put them back into her head. She would then be able to see where the other parts of her body were, and be able to put herself back together again. As it was, she knew she would just have to lie there forever.

Flying and falling dreams often come into the nightmare category and are extremely common examples of anxiety dreams. Flying often shows a desire to rise above a certain situation, but can refer to looking at the big picture. Falling implies an unequal struggle and fear of failure. However, this type of dream can also be very pleasurable, especially if you practise lucid dreaming.

As a young girl, a friend of mine had a recurring dream that involved being chased across her garden by a witch, finally getting up enough speed to take to the air, just in the nick of time, only to catch her feet in the telegraph wires and plummet back to earth. She always woke up before landing. She only realised as an adult that this dream accurately reflected her response to being sexually abused by a family member during the course of several years. She wished to rise above her own problems and the obvious way to do it was to tell other people what was happening. However, as with most abuse cases, she was being threatened and bullied by the abuser, who convinced her that her story would not be believed.

The ability to take control of one's dreams is particularly useful when having a nightmare. My father always told me to find a metal tray in my nightmares, sit down on it and it would whisk me to safety. This was a technique he had used all his life and on the rare occasions I have been able to access my tray, it has worked perfectly!

Recurring dreams are not always

nightmares any more than flying and falling dreams are, rather they are trying to tell us that some situation in our lives is repeating itself. Until we can recognise this situation and deal with it constructively, the dream or the nightmare, will recur.

Here is an interesting example of a recurring dream that was also a precognitive dream: A young boy of eight years old became very keen on the idea of the jungle. He read as much as he could about life in the jungle and determined that he would go and live in one when he was grown up. He then had a vivid nightmare where he found himself running down a jungle trail with an unseen monster behind him. He knew he could escape if only he could resist turning around and looking at it.

At a certain point the trail took a right turn, and he knew that, just out of sight around the corner, a big log lay right across the path, and that he needed to get across it safely. In the dream he rounded the corner, saw the log and just as he was about to go over it, he looked over his shoulder at the monster. He woke up, panicking and sweating with fear. This dream recurred every few months throughout his teens and twenties, always ending the same way. He got to know the trail very well indeed; it never really varied. He began to have some control over the dream – he could look at the trees and plants, sometimes he saw parrots and monkeys, but he could never stop himself from ruining his chance of escape at the last minute by looking over his shoulder.

He landed himself a job as a driver for a trekking company – driving small groups around Africa and South America for six months at a time. Travel was what he had always wanted to do, although by now he had a rather ambivalent attitude to the jungle. His first trip took him to South America. He and an Indian guide were escorting a group down the Amazon for a few days. The group decided that they wanted to spend a night camping in the jungle. Andy and the guide took them on what seemed to be a long trek, cutting a path with their machetes. They had actually only made a series of dog legs, ending up only about 400 yards from the river.

While the campers were busy getting organised, our subject and the guide decided to slip quickly back to the boat and have a couple of beers themselves. Having had their drinks they got ready to go back to the camp. The guide insisted that they ought to be quick as dusk was falling and that he should keep close behind him otherwise he could get lost.

As they set off on yet another trail, the young man suddenly recognised it as the one from his dream and was immediately overcome by panic. His adrenaline surged, his heart pounded and he was terrified. The guide was going very fast and he had to struggle to keep up with him. The path turned to the right and there, just as he had known it would be, was a big log lying across the path. By this point he felt completely paranoid. He thought a jaguar might attack him from behind; he thought the guide might attack him with his machete. However he ploughed on, got over the log, and was soon safely back at the camp.

He was very shaken by this experience, but he has never had that dream again. His ambivalence about jungles vanished and he ended up spending several months living in a tribal village in Brazil, a time he remembers as being the most profound experience of his life.

TRUE DREAMS

This category of dreams includes the rare occasions when the dreamer glimpses the future. They are sometimes known as precognitive dreams, and there are many well documented examples of this phenomenon. President Kennedy's death was foretold in a dream. Jung had a series of dreams that foretold the First World War. Adolf Hitler as a young corporal,dreamt he was being suffocated by falling earth. He woke up, ran out of his bunker, and a few minutes later a shell landed on the bunker, killing everyone inside.

People often report dreams where those very close to them suffer an accident, or die, only to wake up to learn that their dream has become reality. When my father, to whom I was very close, was seriously ill in hospital, I had an extremely vivid dream where he was lying back on pillows, asleep. Suddenly he woke up, and looking me straight in the eyes he gave me a brilliant, loving smile. I woke up with a jolt and noted the time but managed to get back to sleep in due course. In the morning the hospital informed us of my father's death, which had indeed occurred at exactly the time I had woken up. There is no reasonable explanation for this kind of true dream, but if you experience one, pay attention. Just imagine, if Hitler had gone back to sleep, the history of the twentieth century would be altogether different.

LIFE-CHANGING DREAMS

This final category of dreams rarely occurs. You might possibly experience one such dream in your lifetime, if at all. It is a dream which seems to speak to you from a higher power, and it will change your life forever. Many of the prophets of the great religions had life-changing dreams – Jacob, for example, who saw a ladder that stretched from the earth's surface up to heaven, with angels walking up and down it. Mohammed, the prophet of Islam, received the *Koran* from an archangel who dictated it to him, naming him the Messenger of God. It is not only the religious, however, who are visited by these 'big' dreams, it is often the thinkers – philosophers, writers and artists – people to whom

the life of the mind takes precedence
over the daily routine which dominates
so many of our lives.

•

WAYS OF INTERPRETING DREAMS

*All that we see or seem is
but a dream within a dream.*

Edgar Allan Poe

A DREAM WITHIN A DREAM

•

The techniques that are described here are all light-hearted ones that you can perform by yourself or with friends. There are other, more serious methods that are used by therapists and analysts to help those who are emotionally fragile, traumatised or mentally ill. If you have really serious problems, self-help will not be sufficient, and you should seek advice from a professional.

To begin with, you have to try to remember your dreams. We have all had marvellously vivid dreams which, on waking, seem to disappear from our minds. We can repeat the dream out loud, or tell our partner, in order to try to 'fix' it in our mind, only to find that by the end of the morning, it has vanished. Before you go to sleep tell yourself firmly, over and over again, that you want to remember your dream when you wake up. Try to concentrate on this wish as you are dropping off and do not get too downhearted if you do not succeed immediately.

Like anything else, even this first step needs practice. You could try to use an object to help you to remember. For example, place something beside your bed that you would not normally have there. It could be a shell, a crystal, or a teddy bear. Concentrate on it before you go to sleep and tell yourself that when you wake up and see it, you will recall your dream.

When you do remember a dream, write it down. Even this is easier said than done – you may wake up at four in the morning with your mind full of a dream, but be unwilling to wake up sufficiently to pick up a pen. This really is the first step. You have to force yourself to do it the first few times, but it soon becomes an automatic response, and you will be able to go back to sleep without difficulty. You may find that you are writing down nonsense. Don't worry, it will all get easier as time goes on. Soon you will write quite clear accounts.

If you sleep alone you can use a dictaphone or a tape recorder, but this would be rather uncivilised behaviour if you have a partner. In that case you can turn on the light, and write your dream down using the pen and pad you have placed conveniently beside you, or alternatively you can use a torch if your partner is sensitive to light. To begin with, just write down the major points of your dream. You can come back to it later and fill in the detail. If you put down too much detail early on, you may find that the main story vanishes before you have even reached the halfway point. Once you begin to remember more of your dreams, you could start a dream diary and later on in the book I will discuss this in more detail.

You will want to work on explaining your dream to yourself and by now you will quickly realise whether or not there is something to be learnt from it. Remember that we all have lots of dreams which are very mundane – almost re-runs of our days. There are a great many dream symbols which you can use to help in your interpretation, but do not forget that some people, places and objects will have a particular significance for you, which will not appear in any dictionary of symbols. The dictionaries of dream symbols that you can find are really only aids to help you interpret your dreams – you can look up the same word in three different books and find three different interpretations. Dream working is by no means an exact science but we can all recognise the direct messages that our unconscious minds sometimes give us.

Once you get into the habit of remembering and working on your dreams, you can begin to incubate them. Incubation is the name for the technique of asking your dream to answer a question for you. You might want to find a way around a problem at work or at home, either practical or emotional. You might feel ill or have an unexplained pain and want to know what is wrong. You might even want to know the meaning of another dream you have had – something that you feel must be significant but which does not make any sense to you.

In order to incubate your dreams you almost have to practise self hypnosis. Basically, you try to seed your unconscious mind with the question before you go to sleep and persuade it that your conscious mind will take the answer seriously. You will probably find that the best way of achieving this is through some little ceremony. You need to be persuaded that the technique will work if you practise it seriously.

What kind of ritual you choose will depend on your personality. Invent a special routine that you perform each time you wish to incubate a dream. You could relax in a long, hot, scented bath by candlelight. You could wear a special item to bed, either nightwear or a bracelet or a necklace. You could use a special set of bed linen, or sleep with a particular stone, crystal, herb or feather beside you, or under your pillow. You could listen to a piece of music that you use only for this purpose.

All these ritual actions are to help open

the mind to the question you are going to put to it. Make sure that your question is very straightforward. Say, for example, you have a job that you like, close to your home, with a good salary, but you find yourself feeling depressed about it although you can't think of one good reason for your depression. Ask your dreams 'Please tell me why work is depressing me.' Your answer might be that you instinctively distrust your boss, or it might be that although you like your job, what you really want is to go back into further education and study anthropology at university. Be sure to ask your dream why your work is depressing you. If you just ask why you are depressed, you could get a far more general answer, for example, that too many people still die of starvation every year – something which probably depresses most people when they think about it.

Write your question down, maybe even tie it with a special ribbon and put it under your pillow. Say it to yourself as well, at least three times as this allows the question to sink into your unconscious mind. Tell yourself to remember your dream as you drift off to sleep and write it down in the usual way. Make your interpretation and be alert for 'coincidences' that may occur during the course of the next few days. Remember that your answer may come in an incomprehensible way, or may not be an answer that you want to hear. If you receive an answer that you truly disapprove of, do not follow its advice. If you do not receive any answer at all, re-incubate your dream again after a few days.

Do not expect this technique to 'work' immediately. You are attempting to train your unconscious mind, and obviously, this is going to take quite some doing. The reward, if and when it comes, is that your sleeping time becomes far more valuable and interesting to you as you start to explore another plane of consciousness, an alternative universe.

Another technique for exploring your dreams is to set up a dream group. You should decide on one person to be the group leader, either until she/he decides to stop for a while, or you could agree on a change of leader every six sessions. You might want to meet once a month for an evening where you can listen to and discuss one another's dream experiences. The leader can move the discussions along, and bring the group back to the main subject if they have strayed too far, for too long. You should agree not to discuss one another's dreams outside your meetings – dreams are often too personal to be the subject of gossip.

You could find someone who works with dreams to come and talk to you. Better still, find various people with different perspectives, from psychoanalysts to new-agers. You could spend a few sessions acting out your dreams – the action to be directed by the dreamer.

This is quite an interesting exercise with dreams that either you just can't understand but feel strongly are significant, or with dreams that were significant but had no conclusion. You could try to make an object that you have seen in your dreams and that seems to be important – draw or paint a view or a building, reproduce a pattern, frame it and hang it on your wall.

Working with dream symbols can be more interesting than just buying a dictionary of dream symbols from your local bookshop and looking things up. Although this is quite fun, it is of limited use. You should use the dream dictionaries as a starting point for your own dream working. The significance of objects in your dreams depends on many things. For example, if you remember an oak tree, was it in full leaf or was it bare? Could you see acorns? Was it in the background or the foreground of your dream, or were you, perhaps, sitting in the crook of one of its branches, actually touching and being touched by it?

This is another useful reason for learning to have some control over your dreams. You can teach yourself to have a really good look around your dreamscapes instead of just being swept

along by events. Use your dream diary
to work out how often a particular
symbol, person or place crops up in
your dreams over a period of months
and you will soon see who or what is
really occupying your innermost
thoughts.

You can visit your library and begin
researching this symbol's relevance. See
if you can find references to it in
different mythologies – ancient Greece,
Rome and Egypt, Scandinavia, and
North and South America. You can
search through the great religions,
Hindu, Buddhist, Moslem, Jewish and
Christian. Look through art books and
encyclopaedias. Make a list of all the
associations that the object has for you.
Bear in mind that dreams can present

you with puns and double meanings. In this way you may be able to find different levels of meaning to your dreams and besides, you may happen upon a subject that really interests you and sets you on a new path. It may be in this way that an answer comes to an incubated dream.

There are many different types of dream, and there are as many different techniques that you can practise to help control and understand your dreams, and therefore, yourself. You are trying to build a bridge between your conscious and subconscious minds, and to learn a language to ease communication between them both. This may seem almost impossible, but by starting with the simplest technique

and persevering over a period of
months or years you should find that
your new awareness may help you
resolve long-standing difficulties.

KEEPING A DREAM DIARY

To die, to sleep; to sleep:
perchance to dream:
ay, there's the rub;
For in that sleep of death
what dreams may come.

William Shakespeare

HAMLET

It is quite easy to keep a dream diary, and it can be very interesting to look back on. All you need is a notebook or a pad, big enough to have plenty of room to write on. At the top of the page, put the date, and write a little synopsis of your day, including your feelings about what happened. If you decide to incubate a dream, put down your question. Otherwise leave a line to record the type of dream. Leave a reasonable space in which to write your dream. Underline or highlight every element that is relevant – people, animals, objects, buildings, words, journey, colours, weather, atmosphere, your feelings and anything else you think is important. Then try to work out what it is your dream is referring to, or what you think it is telling you.

Here are a few examples and my interpretations to give you an idea of how to make connections between traditional dream symbols and your intuitive insights.

I dreamt that the **garage** at the corner of my road had been turned into a **restaurant**. It was the sort of unpretentious place that I like – big windows at the front, **wooden** floorboards, wooden tables and chairs, and climbing **plants**. It was busy with lots of **people enjoying themselves** and waiters bustling about. **I** found myself at one end, **playing the violin**. In my dream I knew that I cannot play the violin in real life, but there **the music was flying** from the instrument. In fact the music was forming a *physical cord* that was whipping around at the end of my bow. It was an *exhilarating* experience and I woke up feeling wonderful.

My interpretation: The garage which I thought of as cold, dirty and grim was transformed into a lovely, jolly restaurant. A restaurant suggests nourishment, sociability, and communication. (I am very interested in cooking, and frequently have people staying and eating with me in my house. I think it is of particular relevance to my life.) The decor of wood and plants suggests growth, naturalness and warmth, and interior decor usually refers to the dreamer's own qualities. I was able to play this wonderful instrument and the music flew visibly from my bow.

Music concerns emotions, and the type of music, in this case free and soaring, is telling. The violin is often thought to symbolise the female body, and all instruments refer to harmony. All in all, the dream tells me that I am entering a good time in my life, that I am happy in myself, that I am growing as a person, and that I have some creative force that I should definitely nurture.

This is the dream of a thirteen year old girl called Clare who lived in a north American city which was strongly Catholic although she was not a Catholic herself. She was sitting on a bench that in real life she passed every day on her way to school. Suddenly *a very elegant man approached her*. He was dressed in formal, black clothes, and had the beautiful, aquiline features of a Native North-American, but he was the *Devil* and he was *blue*. He politely asked if Clare would like to have *lunch* with him, and she said she would be delighted. An entrance opened up in the pavement beside the bench, and in they went. They were in a very slow lift which went *down and down* into the centre of the earth, where they stopped and got out into a *dining-room*.The dining room was dug out of the earth, and was low ceilinged, warm and humid. They had a very pleasant lunch, and an amusing conversation, waited on by small devils with *forked tails*. At the end of the meal the blue Devil escorted Clare back up to her bench on the earth's surface again. She thanked him very much, and he bowed politely to her and said, 'We shall meet again.'

The Devil represents her animal instincts and also her need to accept that side of herself. Blue symbolises her unconscious mind and also refers to emotions and peace. It can be seen as cold. Falling, but in a controlled way, suggests the need to let go and of the transition to something new. Eating meals always refer to nourishing your basic instincts. The dining-room symbolises emotional nourishment and communication. The little devil's tails are not only symbolic of the Devil but they are also a sexual symbol. The fact that they are forked suggests different directions.

My interpretation: This is a young girl becoming aware of sex and dreaming about her own sexuality, about which she has some fears. The Devil is usually thought of as representing bad things, however, as the whole atmosphere of the dream was adventurous, fun and pleasant, the indications are very positive.

This is the dream of Sophie, a woman in her thirties: she was out with **her young son** on a wonderful day. They were hand-in-hand, walking up a **steep, green hill**. At the top of the hill there was a **blue, sparkling lake**. As she was hot and tired after the walk, she decided to go for a swim, and dived in. The water was cool and transparent and felt lovely. Suddenly she bumped into someone else in the lake, and looking through the water saw it was a

dead body, holding a dead baby.
Swimming closer, she realised it was
herself.

My interpretation: Sophie had been
facing all sorts of difficulties and
problems, but she, together with her
son, had successfully made the
transition from one way of life to
another. The hill represents the
difficulties and water represents
emotions. In dreams it is generally
thought that when you look into water,
or glass, etc., you see yourself. This
woman moved from the hot climb into
a cool lake, and the self and dead baby
that she met there were her old self in
her other life. In fact, Sophie had finally
managed to move back to her own
country after years of a difficult

marriage in another culture. She had found a job, a flat, a school for her son and was filing for divorce.

This is the dream of Kevin, an investment banker in his fifties: he dreamt that he was running along the top of the Sussex downs, jumped off the edge of a mountain and **began to fly around**. He soon realised that **he could control his flight**, and was really enjoying swooping about, when he noticed there was a large **swarm of bees above him**. He immediately started to lose altitude, but then saw that **beneath** him, on the ground, was a large **herd of bullocks**, rushing about all over the place. He flew on, taking care to keep between the bees and the bullocks. Then he saw a **barn and a big field** and started **herding the bullocks** into it. When they were all inside, he flew down and landed on the barn roof. He looked up and saw that **all the bees had gone.**

My interpretation: The controlled flight and enjoyment it brought suggest lucid dreaming, but at the same time, flying represents trying to rise above something, or trying to take an over all view. Bees are active, industrious creatures, who constantly work as part of a team. Being slightly threatened by them suggests a problem with working in a team. The bullocks represent male drives, and in the dream the potentially dangerous bullocks are herded into a safe enclosure, and Kevin lands safely on the roof, which represents both security and the intellect. The bees vanish. I think this is a dream about business. Kevin is safely negotiating his path through possible dangers. He may have a problem with the people who make up his 'team', or possibly with another company and he has to keep himself and the situation, firmly under control. By using his brain he hopes his problem will disappear.

In fact, Kevin was in the midst of complex negotiations with various different people all of whom were bidding for his company.

TRADITIONAL
DREAM SYMBOLS
AND THEIR
INTERPRETATIONS

A

Abbey:
This symbolises peace, meditation and spiritual life, the road to self-knowledge.

Abdomen:
When you dream of a specific part of the body, it suggests you should have your doctor check you.

Abduction:
This symbolises your desire to escape from a person or situation that you cannot seem to get out of.

Abroad:
This could just be a straightforward, wish-fulfilment dream, or it could

mean that you are going through an unsettled stage.

Accelerator:
This symbolises your ambition. You are driven to achieve something, and you do not want anything to get in your way. If you have a nightmare in which your foot gets stuck on the accelerator, it suggests that you should be careful about a bad habit.

Ache:
Dreaming of an ache suggests that you are sleeping in an uncomfortable position. If that is not the case, perhaps you should see your doctor.

Achievement:
This usually means you will have a

success. If, in the dream, you receive a lot of applause, you may be becoming too pleased with yourself. You should be careful not to make a mistake.

Acid:
This is meant as a warning to you. There will be broken promises or broken relationships.

Acorn:
Traditionally seen as a phallic symbol, the acorn augurs success and abundance.

Acrobat:
The context of the dream is important here. You might have to be very flexible about something. You might have to be very agile physically or mentally. You might be taking a risk.

Adoption:
This means there is something
missing in your life and you should
give some thought to what it is you
really want for the future.

Aeroplane:
If you are the pilot this usually means
you are going to be spearheading
some new project. If you could see
where you you were flying, were you
going in a direct line or were you
following a winding path? Were you
being flown by someone else? Was it
a smooth flight or not? Aeroplanes are
also phallic symbols and the project
could be sexual.

Alphabet:
Dreaming of letters, if they appear to

be in another language, means you are looking for the meaning of something which you do not understand. Your own alphabet, jumbled, means the brain is busy with abstract thoughts. Occasionally you can read a word or a phrase. Try to work out what it could mean for you. Don't forget that the mind produces puns as well as metaphors.

Ancestors:
You must listen to the message they are sending you. Your ancestors represent different sides of yourself. You are telling yourself something important that your conscious mind does not yet know.

Animals:
Animals can represent different things.

Think about what each animal represents – dogs we tend to think of as friends, pigs as dirty, bulls as male, tigers as wild, birds as free. The animal's behaviour and attitude in the dream is also pertinent.

Arena:
This symbolises a risky situation. You are highly visible and either alone or with a potential enemy.

Armchair:
This represents something safe and comfortable. It could be a warning that you are getting lazy. If you see someone else in your armchair you should beware that someone is trying to move into some area of your life. If you are with someone else and they are in their

own armchair, you see them as being in a powerful position.

Arrow:
Dreaming of an arrow means you are concentrating hard on one specific thing. This may point to romance and it is a phallic symbol.

Assassination:
This is an anxiety dream. It implies that you feel as though you have an enemy and that you are in danger. You must remain alert but you are afraid it may be too late.

Attic:
This represents your spiritual side. Attics are generally where we store things we do not use every day, but

that we value enough to want to keep safe. We store thoughts and feelings that we do not want to look at too closely and those we do not want others to see. Try to remember if you could see anything in your attic, and if so, try to remember what it was. Think about what it might represent to you. Was the attic clean,tidy and well lit or dusty and full of cobwebs?

Autumn:
If it is a golden autumn day, this represents a sense of mellowness and security in your life. If it is a grey, gloomy day it can signify that a relationship is reaching a natural conclusion.

B

Baby:
Babies are thought to represent your creative instincts. If the infant is thriving, you are doing well, but if something bad happens to it, there is a latent talent that you are not nurturing. If you are the baby, it suggests that you are feeling helpless and want to be taken care of.

Back:
If you only see someone's back in your dream, or someone turns their back on you, you should take it as a warning sign. There may be someone who is hiding something from you or someone who is turning away from you. It could be a metaphor for feeling that your back is against the wall, you are being stabbed

in the back, you should back down.

Baldness:
If you dream of being bald it points to
some perceived lack of intelligence.
Baldness in a friend suggests you are
being cheated by someone. Suddenly
going bald is another anxiety dream,
similar to finding your teeth
crumbling.

Bank:
This suggests some unexpected good
fortune, if you dreamt you were
putting money into the bank.
Withdrawing money is a warning to
take care of your finances.

Barefoot:
Unlike being completely naked, being

barefoot in your dream shows that you are properly grounded, having your feet firmly on the ground. If the dream is romantic or sexual, it could be a metaphor for being swept off your feet, or of being footloose and fancy-free.

Barrel:
If the barrel is full, it suggests a time of plenty, but if it is leaking or empty it suggests that hard times are coming, and you should take steps to secure your position.

Basement:
We are all accustomed to the idea of there being monsters waiting for us in the dark, down in the basement. It is the place of nightmares. It is where we chuck things that we do not want or

like, including unpleasant thoughts and deeds. It may mean that you have something on your conscience that you should deal with.

Bath:
Dreams of water are usually thought to be sexual but dreams of bathing are often also about cleansing yourself, scrubbing away dirt. Luxuriating in a warm bath implies sexual contentment. If the water is too hot, or too cold, it suggests you may be getting into something that you are not happy about.

Bedroom:
To dream of your bedroom is usually to dream of safety and privacy. You may find yourself in bed with another person, or people, in a non-sexual way, which

suggests you trust them and feel close to them. Erotic dreams are more concerned with eroticism than the room or bed itself.

Bees and Beehives:
These dreams usually signify co-operation and hard work being rewarded.

Bell:
Peals of bells are traditionally seen as being a good omen but a single bell can be read as an attempt by your subconscious to get the attention of your conscious mind and make you aware of something you need to know.

Bicycle:
Bicycles represent your independence,

going your own way, under your own steam. Think about what kind of bicycle it was, old or new? Were you speeding along or pushing it up a hill?

Birthday:
Dreaming of your own birthday, or that of another, is a symbol of good luck. It is a celebration of your own life, and the presents you receive are symbolic of different aspects of your own character.

Blood:
This symbolises the life force, energy and passion. Loss of blood indicates something is going seriously wrong. It could be a metaphor for someone bleeding you dry, or making your blood boil or run cold.

Book:
This symbolises a tranquil inner life, and a desire to learn and to become wiser. You could be taking stock of your life so far. If you can remember a book title, it will be significant.

Bridge:
This is usually a symbol of change, of crossing from one thing to another. The bridge is often over a chasm or a rushing river, implying taking a chance. If you cross the bridge successfully, you have taken a real step forward in your life, made an important decision.

Broadcast:
If you dream that you are broadcasting a programme it symbolises your desire to put your full weight behind

something. You are fully committed and quite prepared to stand by your decision.

Broom:
This is another symbol of cleaning. You may need to clean up an area of your life, sweep away the cobwebs. Brooms also suggest witchcraft, and are phallic symbols.

Building:
A building represents yourself. Many people have recurring dreams that feature the same building each time, although as you begin to go inside it and explore, new rooms can suddenly appear. The facade of the building represents the facade that you present to the world. Therefore if it is

in a poor state, you may be letting yourself go physically, or you may be depressed about the way you look. If the building is actually falling down, you could visit your doctor for a check up. If the building is in good condition, that is a very good sign.

Burglar:
This suggests that you feel someone is invading your territory. This could be at work or in a relationship. You are frightened of losing something. Of course, this just could be a precognitive dream, so it might be sensible to check your security systems.

Bus:
This symbolises your journey through life, as it is presently. It suggests that

you are working collectively rather than alone, and that your aims are for the communal good.

Butterfly:
Dreaming of butterflies is symbolic of the spirit's lightness and childlike joy. It can also imply a new beginning.

❧

C

Cage:
If you dream of being inside a cage,
you are feeling imprisoned, but if you
are looking at one from the outside, it
suggests that you feel quite safe and
that your wild and dangerous thoughts
and feelings are safely contained. Two
birds in a cage is thought to symbolise
romance.

Camera:
A camera implies that you are focusing
on something in your life that needs to
be looked at more objectively. You
should stand back from it. You are
seeing one image rather than the
whole picture. You are not wholly
involved.

Cannibal:
You need to give or receive more space
in a relationship which is becoming too
intense.

Car:
You should pay attention to a number
of different things when you dream of a
car. The car represents yourself, and
travelling represents your journey
through life. The car might be a sports
car, a rusty old banger or a stretch
limo. Are you the driver or the
passenger? Perhaps no-one is driving it
and it is out of control. Is it a particular
colour? Can you see the numberplate?
Are you inside it or just looking at it?

Cards:
Playing cards signifies either that you

are taking risks in your life or that you need to take things a little less seriously. Different cards represent different things – for example, the Jack of Hearts represents a new man in your life. Are you holding good or bad cards? Business or credit cards suggest that you want to be successful.

Carpenter:
This is a positive image of which to dream. You are shaping and building yourself and your life, and have a good self-image.

Cat:
Cats always refer to your feminine side. They traditionally represent cunning, independence and freedom. They are also a symbol for female genitalia.

Ceiling:
This usually represents your intellect. If
the ceiling is very high, it implies you
are overstretching your mind. If the
ceiling is too low, your mind needs to
be stretched.

Church:
This symbolises peace, harmony and
quiet contemplation.

Clown:
If you are the clown it suggests that you
fear you are making a fool of yourself.
If you are watching a clown it suggests
you should try to have some fun.

Court:
If you find yourself up in court in your
dream, it suggests that you are judging

yourself. You may well have a guilty conscience or feel ashamed of yourself.

Crab:
This is an astrological symbol for the sign of Cancer. It represents several things – its claws can be threatening, it scuttles along sideways and it lives partly on land and partly in the sea. The shoreline represents the dividing line between our intellects and our emotions. You could have had a true dream, as obviously the crab can also be symbol of illness, this suggests that you should visit your doctor.

Curtain:
This suggests something is being hidden from you, or that you want to hide something from yourself.

D

Dance:
This is usually a woman's dream and it symbolises the rhythm of life to which women are closely attuned. Dancing in your dreams is a joyous, thrilling experience, your body and mind are working in perfect harmony, with or without a partner. A dream to cherish.

Death:
There are many types of dreams of death but it is thought to symbolise the end of one thing and the beginning of something else. It is extremely unlikely to foretell your own imminent death. It can apply to people, situations or emotions. You should try to remember who it was that died, and what you felt

about it. It might be telling you a relationship has run its course or that you want to move house. It could also be part of the grieving process.

Devil:
The Devil represents the darker, animal side of ourselves – the side we do not always want to acknowledge.

Dirt:
Dreaming that everything is dirty usually suggests that you feel unclean in some way. You may find yourself in some situation that you are not happy with, in a relationship, in your work or even sexually.

Door:
A door usually symbolises the start of

something new. Closed doors represent
chances missed. Doors are also
symbolic of female genitalia.

Dragon:
Dragons are a symbol of great good
luck and wealth to come. If the dragon
was aggressive it can refer to your fear
of a woman.

Drink:
Usually, if you drink in your dreams, it
just means that you are thirsty.

Drowning:
This suggests a sense of helplessness,
that you are being overwhelmed. Water
dreams are connected to emotions, and
you feel you are being submerged
under their weight.

Drums:
If you hear drums in your dreams it suggests something new and exciting is about to start.

Dust:
This suggests feelings of insecurity, about yourself, or another. It could also suggest that a business venture or new relationship is not as solid as it appears.

Dwarf:
If you are the dwarf, your dream suggests that you feel small and helpless, surrounded by a world that is much larger and stronger than you.

E

Ear:
This suggests that you need to pay closer attention to what is being said to you. You should also listen more attentively to yourself. The ear is a symbol of female sexuality. If you are dreaming of an ear of wheat, it is symbolic of fertility and abundance.

Earthquake:
If you live in an earthquake zone, you may be having a precognitive dream, and you might contact your nearest seismology centre. Normally this would be a severe insecurity dream, probably as a result of an emotional trauma such as the death of a parent or partner, or the collapse of your

business. It therefore signifies the start of a new way of life.

Eel:
The eel is a classic sexual symbol. A feeling of disgust in your dream suggests sexual problems.

Embarrassment:
This is an insecurity dream. Perhaps you feel that you alone hold some conviction. It could also imply that you are aware of being at fault in something.

Emerald:
This is symbolic of great good fortune but it can also signify vanity.

Escalator:
It is important to remember if you were

going up or coming down, indicating success or failure.

Evening:
This usually means that you are over stressed and feel in need of a break.

Exam:
Being unprepared for an exam suggests that you are going through a difficult period in your life and if you fail it, you are having problems with your self-esteem. If you sail through it the implication is clear.

Execution:
To see an execution suggests that you need to make drastic changes to some of your current behaviour. It suggests putting an end to something. If you are

the person being executed, you are probably consumed by guilt and you should deal with it.

Eyes:
The eyes are thought of as the windows of the soul. If you dream of eyes, there may be something important that you are not allowing yourself to see. If you see yourself in a dream, and look into your own eyes, it suggests that you need to have a good look at who you really are.

F

Face:
The expression on a face in your dream reflects your own emotions. Is the face angry or fearful, calm or smiling? Traditionally, a happy face is a good omen and a sad one is not.

Fame:
This suggests ambition and a desire to be recognised. If you dream of a famous person, think about their most obvious characteristics. This is a pointer to an aspect of yourself that you want to work on.

Fire:
This usually represents your own passionate emotions. It could be that

you fear their destructive properties or it could be that you yearn to unleash them.

Floor:
This represents your own bottom line. You are safe, grounded, the floor is solid, immoveable. When we have nightmares in which the floor suddenly disappears, or we fall through it, it is indicative of severe insecurity.

Flower:
Flowers traditionally represent our emotions – red roses for love, for example. They are also symbolic of female genitalia.

Fog:
Dreaming of fog suggests that

something is going on, in your life or in your sub-conscious, that you cannot quite understand. It needs to be brought into the clear light of day and examined properly.

Forest:
This usually represents our unconscious selves. Forests are often dark and mysterious, sometimes frightening places. Walking in a forest suggests an attempt to explore your innermost self.

Fragrance:
To dream of a gorgeous smell is unusual. Perhaps you were smelling it in real life? If you were actually dreaming, it suggests your sensual nature is vibrant and strong. Fragrances can remind you incredibly strongly of a particular place

or person, so perhaps you were actually thinking of something or someone specific.

Fruit:
Fruit represents sexuality, fertility and abundance. Rotten fruit suggests illness.

Fur:
This depends on what sort of fur you dream about. If it is a luxurious fur coat, it suggests self-admiration and vanity. It might also suggest that you disapprove strongly of something you are doing. It might just mean that you are feeling cold. If you dream of an animal, think of what it represents – cuddly, fierce and so on.

ॐ

G

Garden:
This represents a place close to nature, abundance, fertility, growth and peace. It is the domestic, tamed part of your nature and the opposite of the dark, mysterious forest.

Ghost:
A ghost often represents your conscience. Perhaps you have done something you feel guilty about. It depends on your sense of the ghost – is it frightening or is it trying to help you in some way? It could mean that something or someone you believe in is just a mirage.

Glass:
Glass containers represent your

spirituality. It can also suggest an unseen barrier between yourself and someone else. A broken glass is a bad omen.

Glue:
This is a straightforward symbol of wishing to repair something. Perhaps you have quarrelled with a friend, or split up with a partner. If you are glued to something or someone, perhaps you are feeling trapped.

Goodbye:
Saying goodbye suggests that you must or you have moved on from something or someone important to you. You are letting go of something.

Government:
This signifies authority. Perhaps you feel

that you are being controlled by other people, or perhaps it means that you want to be in control and authority yourself.

Grandparents:
They represent the all-powerful mother and father images, but with the emphasis on the past. They often appear to be immensely wise. Their appearance in your dream suggests that you are in a pattern of behaviour that can be altered only if you look for answers from your past.

Guard:
This suggests you are on the defensive, guarding your thoughts, watching your back. You could be guarding your thoughts against yourself – perhaps you

are thinking about or feeling something that you do not want to deal with, or that you know is wrong.

Gun:
Dreaming of guns suggests that you feel threatened or frightened. Guns almost always appear in nightmares. A gun is also a strong phallic symbol.

Gypsy:
This usually represents your wild and romantic side. It shows a desire to be irresponsible and free. It can also imply feelings of not fitting in, of being an outsider.

H

Harbour:
This is a symbol of security, of being protected from dangerous forces. If you are leaving the harbour this suggests you are stepping into uncharted waters, and you must be alert.

Harem:
Whether you dream of living in one as a woman or visiting one as a man, this dream concerns sexuality. You may be sexually inhibited or frustrated, or you might just be enjoying an unusually active sex life.

Haste:
'More haste, less speed.' This saying is almost always true in our dreams. We

are rushing somewhere, getting more
and more anxious about the time, and
never quite arriving. Time, in dreams,
is about our own limitations, so this
type of dream is about a fear of failure.

Hat:
Dreaming of hats, or indeed heads, is
connected to the intellect. Perhaps you
are using your mind so much that you
are neglecting the other areas of your
life. Hats also imply arrogance and
vanity – the type of hat in your dream
symbolises some aspect of your
personality.

Hell:
This is the classic symbol for sin and
suggests you have a very bad
conscience about something. Perhaps

you are getting involved in something of which you really do not approve, 'selling your soul' in other words.

Highway:
Highways, roads, tracks and paths are all symbolic of life's journey and are connected with the present time. Is the highway smooth and clear or is it rutted and crowded? Are you in a vehicle or on foot? Going fast or slow?

History:
Our gene pool gives us access to the experiences of all the generations of people who came before us and so if you dream of living in another age it is possible that you are experiencing a far memory dream. If you dream of a famous historical character you should

try to do some research on him/her and see what relevance there is to your own life.

Hospital:
This is a sign that you feel you need to be helped and looked after in your emotional life. The illness you dream of may reflect your problem. You might possibly be dreaming of a real illness, and should perhaps visit your doctor if the dream keeps recurring.

House:
Houses represent our essential selves, and everything about them is relevant. The repair they are in, both outside and within; the individual rooms and their contents; whether the doors and windows are opened or closed, every

aspect is important. Do you frequently dream of the same house? Do you sometimes find new rooms?

Hunger:
If you dream that you are hungry, it usually means that you are actually hungry. However, if that is not the case, then the hunger may be symbolic of intellectual or emotional hunger.

I

Ice:
This indicates frozen emotions, a
barrier between your mind and your
heart. Dreaming that ice gives way
beneath your feet means you are fearful
of failing. It could also mean that you
are having difficulty achieving orgasm.

Idiot:
The Idiot or Fool is a traditional
symbol for a wise man. 'Fools rush in
where angels fear to tread.' The Idiot
suggest you should look at a situation
laterally. Another kind of idiot, a foolish
person, suggests that you think either
you are being stupid about something
or that someone else is fooling you.

Incest:

Dreams of being in bed with inappropriate people are quite frequent, but dreaming of an incestuous lover requires serious thought. It could just point to a very close bond that you have with a relative, but it could be that you find the relationship threatening. Recurring dreams of father/daughter or mother/son incest might mean you should seek professional help.

Insects:
Insect dreams are almost always unpleasant, and imply a fear of being overcome by some alien force against which you are powerless.

Intercourse:
Sexual dreams are usually quite straightforward. They usually refer to

your desire for sex, or for a particular partner, or they can just be in response to a physical reaction in your sleeping body.

Island:
An island in your dreams refers to yourself. It implies self-sufficiency and independence, or a desire for them. It can also suggest loneliness and feelings of separation.

J

Jacket:
This refers to the way you want to present yourself to the world, the way you want to be seen. The appearance of the jacket is meaningful, as is its condition.

Jewellery:
Dreaming of wearing jewellery implies vanity and personal ambition. To be given jewellery suggests romance.

Job:
If you dream of a new job, it suggests frustration in your daily life. Perhaps you need to take on new responsibilities, stretch yourself a bit more. It could just be a literal dream,

because your job is occupying a lot of your thoughts.

Joke:
If you are amused by a joke in a dream, try to remember it. The joke may be suggesting an alternative spin on a situation. It might also suggest that you need to lighten up and enjoy yourself a bit more.

Jug:
Jugs are symbolic of female sexuality. If the jug is full, it suggests abundance and fertility, but if it is empty or broken it suggests emotional or sexual problems.

Juggling:
This suggests you are juggling with

different aspects of your life, trying to keep balanced. It could also suggest that you are indecisive.

Jungle:
The jungle represents the difficulties you have in your everyday life, in your emotions, your work and your finances. It suggests you are struggling through some rather frightening situation and that you do not know quite where you are going.

K

Key:
Keys and locks are sexual symbols, and the physical action of locking denotes intercourse. Losing a key is a classic anxiety dream.

Kiss:
This implies a desire for intimate contact with someone. It need not necessarily be a desire for sexual contact, just a desire for closeness. It all depends on the type of kiss, and who the other person is.

Kitchen:
The kitchen represents creativity and nourishment, both physical and emotional. A kitchen is usually a safe,

warm, domestic room and if your dream kitchen is empty, neglected or dirty it suggests you feel unloved and unclean.

Kite:
This is a straightforward dream of success, happiness and general lightness of spirit. It is a bad omen if the kite is hard to fly, the string snaps or it keeps falling back to the ground.

Knife:
A knife is a powerful, male symbol, suggesting aggression and violence. It can also be defensive, but it implies a considerable degree of strong, negative emotions. Traditionally it is said to warn of betrayal, as in a knife in the back.

Knot:
This suggests tangled emotions, or a problem that is difficult solve.

Knitting:
This is a dream of domestic creativity – unless you are a knitter, in which case it could just be a literal dream.

L

Ladder:
This is symbolic of the connection between your conscious and unconscious self and can have spiritual or religious significance. Are you going up the ladder or coming back down? Where is the ladder taking you?

Laughing:
This suggests all sorts of good, positive emotions. Some of the best dreams are those we laugh in, and we wake up feeling terrific. It suggests that you are relaxed, happy and problem-free.

Lecture:
All dreams of public performance are directly related to yourself. If you find

yourself giving a lecture in a dream, it suggests you wish to or are trying to communicate something important. If you are being lectured to, it suggests there is a lesson that you need to learn.

Light:
Lights and lamps represent your consciousness, your intellectual and reasoning ability. It suggests you need to shine the light of reason on your problem.

Lottery:
A typical wish-fulfilment dream is that you have won millions on the lottery. Of course, if you dream of the exact numbers that you won with, it might be worth taking a small gamble!

Luggage:
Luggage is symbolic of carrying an emotional burden. The larger and heavier the luggage, the more burdened you are. You would be advised to try to sort out your difficulties.

Lying:
This suggests that you have a bad conscience about something or that you feel that you are living a lie. If you realise in your dream that you are lying about something, it shows self-awareness. If you realise someone is lying to you it suggests that you are becoming aware of a lack of honesty in a relationship.

~

M

Machine:
This suggests boredom with your daily life, or your job. You are living on automatic pilot, your routine is tedious. You need to do something more creative.

Market:
This refers to your social connections in everyday life. How you deal with them and how they deal with you. The market itself is significant – is it crowded or empty?

Marble:
This symbolises beauty and wealth, but also hardness and coldness. It suggests you are not in touch with your feelings.

Maze:
This suggests that your life is so complicated that you are in danger of getting lost. However, you know that if you follow the path carefully, you will reach the centre, where you will meet your true self.

Medal:
This is a dream about ambition and competition. It also shows a desire to be recognised by your peers, or your colleagues. If you actually receive a medal, it suggests vanity.

Message:
If you are the messenger, it suggests there is something you want to say. If you are receiving a message in your dream, perhaps you should be listening

more carefully. Traditionally it means
that you will hear important news.

Money:
In dreams, money usually represents
power and success or the lack of it or
it could be a simple wish-fulfilment
dream.

Monster:
Monsters represent our own animal
natures. Dreaming of one suggests you
are afraid of your own instincts and
desires.

Mountain:
If you dream of climbing a mountain,
it suggests you are dealing with a
difficult problem. If you are on top of
a mountain admiring the view, it

suggests a desire for solitude and peace.

Music:
Music in dreams symbolises your emotional state, so the music itself is important. Pay attention to how it made you feel.

N

Naked:
Most people, at some time, dream that they are naked in a public place. These dreams reflect your feelings of insecurity and vulnerability. You are afraid everyone can see through you and that you are making yourself ridiculous. Sometimes though, either people do not seem to notice, or you do not care if they do. This implies a shedding of some inhibition.

Net:
Dreaming of a net suggests your connections with others. It could also suggest you are caught up in something, or that you want to catch hold of something or someone.

Nest:
This suggests a dream about security, protection and the home.

Night:
This refers to your unconscious – the unknown, frightening side of yourself. You might benefit from doing some conscious work on yourself.

Number:
If you dream of a particular number of people or objects in your dream, you should try to find out what the significance of that number actually is. If you dream of a sequence of numbers, try to think what possible meaning they could have in your life, as a date or a year. Traditionally the numbers, or some combination of them, should bring you luck.

O

Oasis:
Water in dreams is connected to sexuality and emotions and the type of water (sea, river, bath) and its mood (calm, rough, warm) is very significant. An oasis suggests a beautiful place to be, relaxing and refreshing, in the middle of a desert.

Obedience:
This suggests that either you need someone to take responsibility for you, or that you want more control and authority in your life.

Oil:
This often implies dirt and pollution, but it can also refer to healing and

cleansing. What kind of oil are you dreaming about?

Opening:
Dreaming of an opening suggests a new start in some direction. If you actually go through the opening, can you see where you are? If you can, it might suggest the new direction you should be aiming for.

Ornament:
If you dream of an ornament that you know, you can try to see what it refers to by thinking about where it is and who it belongs to. If it is something you have never seen before, its significance can be inferred from what it actually represents and what it is made from.

Other people:
If your dream is full of other people whom you do not know but with whom you are dealing, it suggests you are working on your self-knowledge. Each of these other people represent a side of yourself.

Oven:
A hot oven symbolises some emotional transformation that is taking place internally. A hot oven points to warm, positive feelings, and a cold, unlit oven suggests the opposite. An oven is also a symbol of female sexuality.

Oyster:
Traditionally oysters are symbolic of female genitalia, but it can also suggest a desire for material goods and a luxurious lifestyle.

P Q

Parachute:
Dreaming of parachuting slowly
downwards is symbolic of letting go,
drifting down gently, possibly falling in
love. It is a really pleasant experience,
and suggests being open and
experimentally creative. A positive
dream. Occasionally, in a nightmare,
the parachute does not open, but this is
a falling dream and not a flying dream.

Paralysis:
Another common nightmare is that of
being chased or threatened by
something, and finding that one is
totally incapable of moving, or even
screaming for help. This is known as
sleep paralysis and is thought to be the

brain's response to a particular level of sleep. Thus the dream is being influenced by the body. The nightmare can sometimes shock you awake, but for a few seconds it is still impossible to move.

Party:
If you dream of being at a party, the meaning of the dream is tied to the ambience of the party. Usually parties are sociable occasions, relaxing and fun, which suggests all is well. If it is a nightmare, you should try to interpret the specifics rather than the party itself – were you naked? Did you find your partner in a compromising situation? Did you get lost? Were all the other guests menacing strangers?

Photograph:
If you see a photograph in your dream, it

probably refers to some event in your own past history. It could be that you need to look at something again now in order to understand it more completely.

Picnic:
Eating dreams refer to spiritual and emotional needs that require nourishment. A picnic should be a peaceful and relaxed occasion at a beautiful site. This suggests romance and sensuality. It could also just mean that you are hungry.

Portrait:
Portraits show you facets of your own character and attitudes even when they are of someone else.

Puppet:
This is a dream that suggests you have some serious problems to deal with. It implies that you feel you are a puppet, that you have no mind or soul of your own, that you are an empty toy, completely controlled by someone or something else. If you have many such dreams, you would probably benefit from counselling.

Q

Quarrel:
This suggests inner turbulence and conflict. Think about what you were quarrelling about, and who you were quarrelling with as this may help clarify your situation.

R

Racing:
This is usually about your competitive instinct, particularly in reference to your career. Are you winning or losing? It suggests that you are under some stress.

Railway:
Railway stations are symbolic of your real life. They suggest you are about to take a new direction. Trains, like other means of transport, refer to your own journey. Are you driving the train yourself, or is someone else? Do you know where you are going and is the journey straightforward or full of obstacles? Are you on the right track?

Rainbow:
It is a very good omen to dream of a rainbow. It is a symbol of unity and harmony that encompasses the world. It is water and fire, two opposites, joining together. Water represents sensuality and fire represents energy and transformation. This is a very positive and creative dream.

Razor:
This refers to the intellect, possibly how to smooth over an argument. Traditionally it warns of trouble ahead.

Referee:
This suggests your own judgement and fairness, or unfairness, towards both yourself and others.

Rejection:
If you suffer rejection in your dream it suggests that you feel insecure and alone. You want closer ties with someone but you are frightened of being shut out.

Riding:
Riding dreams are concerned with sexuality, power, freedom and excitement.

Ring:
If you give or receive a ring in your dream, it suggests you have a close connection with the other person involved. It is a symbol of wholeness. If it is very ornate and made with precious stones, it could imply vanity.

Roof:
The roof shelters the house and the house represents your self. It refers to your conscious thoughts. If your roof is in bad condition it suggests that the situation is becoming out of control.

Rust:
This suggests something is wearing out, crumbling, old. Try to think of what it might be.

∾

S

Sailor:
This is symbolic of restlessness and the desire for adventure and travel. It is also about a need for independence.

Scales:
This symbolises judgement and balance. You are assessing the value of your life as a whole. It suggests you have to reach an important decision.

Servant:
If you are the servant, it suggests that you feel as though you are being pushed around by someone. If there is a servant in your dream, you may be behaving in a high-handed fashion, imposing your own will on other

people. Perhaps you have too high an opinion of yourself.

Shawl:
If you dream of being wrapped in a shawl, it suggests you feel loved and protected as a shawl is symbolic of security.

Shrinking:
A dream in which you shrink suggests you feel smaller than the people around you. You feel that you are being overlooked. It is usually an unpleasant dream.

Smoking:
This is usually dreamt by people who have given up smoking. It can be that they wake up thinking they have been

weak and taken it up again, but it can also be part of a pleasant, social dream, symbolic of relaxation.

Snow:
Snow changes the familiar outlines of the things around you, and muffles sound and it suggests a change of attitude and emotional distance. It could just mean that you are not warm enough.

Sowing:
This is usually a sexual dream symbol, but it can suggest the sowing of new thoughts and ideas.

Speed:
This is usually an anxiety dream, suggesting that things are going very

fast. Perhaps you need to slow down a little.

Statue:
Try to remember who the statue represented. If it was someone famous, make an effort to find out about them, there may be some relevance to your life. If it was of yourself, it suggests that you have too high an opinion of yourself.

Swimming:
This is dream of sensuality, freedom and pleasure. If the water is dirty and the swimming is a struggle it suggests sexual difficulties.

T

Teeth:
Having all your teeth suddenly crumble in your mouth is a very common anxiety dream.

Thief:
This often refers to relationships – do you feel that something or someone is stealing a relationship from you? Or are you suffering from a guilty conscience about doing the stealing yourself?

Thunder:
Thunder usually represents aggressive feelings, and anger. It suggests getting these emotions out into the open, expressing them fully. It could just be that a loud noise has penetrated your dream.

Tongue:
This is suggestive of speech and communication. Are you tongue tied or holding your tongue?

Tower:
This is a traditional phallic symbol. In women's dreams, being locked into a tower suggests domination by a man, and possibly repressed sexual feelings.

Trap:
This is a straightforward dream of feeling caught or trapped in a bad situation.

Tunnel:
This is thought to be a dream of your birth, although if you are entering or

leaving a tunnel it may be suggesting sexual activity.

Twins:
Twins normally represent two different sides of yourself. The self that you present to the world and your inner self. How did the twins behave? Were they identical or very different?

&

U V

Undressing:
This dream usually refers to openness and showing your honest thoughts and feelings. It can be part of a sexual dream.

Unicorn:
The mythical unicorn represents purity, innocence and goodness. The only person who could tame it was a virgin – it would put its horn in her lap. The unicorn's horn can be seen as a phallic symbol.

Vomiting:
This suggests you need to rid yourself of emotions that are choking you.

W Y Z

War:
This suggests either that you are at war
with yourself over something, or feel
very aggressive towards someone else.
It is also quite possible that you have
been disturbed by watching or reading
news reports of an actual war.

Warning:
If you received a warning in your
dream, you should pay attention to it.

Wood:
This is symbolic of closeness to nature,
strength, comfort and warmth.

Writing:
This often means you need to think

about or do something. You are writing yourself a message or a list. Can you read what you have written? Try to find out what it means.

Yoga:
This is a dream about having control over your own body. Perhaps you are overweight or unfit, perhaps you are frightened of your body's needs.

Zoo:
This suggests keeping your animal instincts behind bars.